Understanding the Coronavirus

Understanding COVID-19

Margaret J. Goldstein

Lerner Publications ◆ Minneapolis

Lerner Publications Company
An imprint of Lerner Publishing Group, Inc.
241 First Avenue North
Minneapolis, MN 55401 USA

For reading levels and more information, look up this title at www.lernerbooks.com.

Main body text set in Adrianna Regular.
Typeface provided by Chank.

Library of Congress Cataloging-in-Publication Data

Names: Goldstein, Margaret J., author.
Title: Understanding COVID-19 / Margaret J. Goldstein.
Description: Minneapolis : Lerner Publications , [2022] | Series: Searchlight books - understanding the coronavirus | Includes bibliographical references and index. | Audience: Ages 8–11 | Audience: Grades 2–3 | Summary: "Learn all about COVID-19, including its global spread, social distancing guidelines, and the search for a vaccine. This approachable book will help readers understand the pandemic and answer many of their questions about the disease"—Provided by publisher.
Identifiers: LCCN 2021008059 (print) | LCCN 2021008060 (ebook) | ISBN 9781728428529 (library binding) | ISBN 9781728431499 (paperback) | ISBN 9781728430775 (ebook)
Subjects: LCSH: COVID-19 (Disease)—Juvenile literature. | Coronavirus infection —Juvenile literature. | COVID-19 (Disease)—Social aspects—Juvenile Literature. | COVID-19 (Disease)—Treatment—Juvenile literature.
Classification: LCC RA644.C67 G6476 2022 (print) | LCC RA644.C67 (ebook) | DDC 362.1962/414—dc23

LC record available at https://lccn.loc.gov/2021008059
LC ebook record available at https://lccn.loc.gov/2021008060

Manufactured in the United States of America
1-49389-49493-4/26/2021

Table of Contents

Chapter 1

VIRUS ALERT

In 2020, a deadly virus spread around the world. The virus emerged in China at the end of 2019. Then international travelers carried it to other nations. Scientists studied the virus to learn more about it. They discovered it was a coronavirus, a name that means "crown virus."

Each virus particle is covered by little spikes. They look like points on a crown. A team of international scientists gave the virus an official name, SARS-CoV-2, but the media simply called it the coronavirus. The virus caused a disease called COVID-19.

The spikes on the coronavirus lock into cells in the human body.

Most people who are infected with the coronavirus have mild symptoms, such as coughs, fevers, and body aches. They usually recover on their own at home. Some people who got the virus didn't get sick at all. But others became extremely sick. They had trouble breathing and needed hospital care. Many of those patients died.

BECAUSE THE VIRUS ATTACKS THE LUNGS, COUGHING IS A COMMON SYMPTOM OF COVID-19.

STEM Spotlight

A pandemic is a widespread outbreak of disease. Pandemics have hit human society many times before. One of the worst pandemics took place in 1918 and 1919. A deadly flu virus spread around the world. At the time, there was no flu vaccine. Doctors then didn't know much about viruses. They did not have good medicines to treat the sick. Worldwide, the virus infected about 500 million people and killed at least 50 million. In the United States, the virus killed about 675,000 people.

Going Global

As the virus moved from country to country, health agencies tracked its spread. They noted how many people were infected, how many people went to the hospital, and how many died. Around the world, numbers of COVID-19 cases rose and fell in different places at different times. But the virus kept infecting more and more people. By February 2021, it had infected more than 100 million people worldwide and had killed more than 2 million.

By February 2021, the US death toll from COVID-19 totaled more than 500,000 people.

In memory of the 200,000+ Americans who have needlessly lost their lives to COVID-19

#COVIDMemorialProject

Chapter 2

PLAYING IT SAFE

The virus that causes COVID-19 spreads from person to person. When an infected person sneezes, coughs, talks, or even just breathes, they release virus-filled droplets into the air. People standing nearby can inhale the droplets and get infected too. Droplets might land on a surface, such as a desk or a doorknob. If someone else touches that surface and then touches their mouth or nose, the virus can enter their body.

The Centers for Disease Control and Prevention (CDC) recommends that children over the age of two wear masks in public.

When the coronavirus started spreading, doctors and other health experts issued warnings. They told people to wear face masks that covered the nose and mouth. Masks help keep virus-filled droplets from passing from one person to another. Health professionals also recommended that people stand at least 6 feet (2 m) away from others. They said frequent handwashing with soap or hand sanitizer would help to remove virus particles on the skin.

Shutdown

Health agencies also told people to avoid crowds. Sports leagues worried that fans and players might infect one another, so they canceled games and tournaments. Organizers canceled music festivals and concerts. Many businesses shut their offices. They had employees work from home using personal computers and online tools. Many schools switched to online learning. Instead of going to doctors' offices, many patients talked to their doctors on video chats.

To stay safe from COVID-19, workers use online platforms to have meetings from home.

Jana De Brauwere

Jana De Brauwere is a COVID-19 contact tracer in San Francisco, California. In this job, she talks to people who are infected with the coronavirus. She asks for names and phone numbers of their friends, family members, coworkers, and others they've spent time with. These contacts might be infected too. De Brauwere encourages those people to get tested for the virus. If they are already sick with COVID-19, she encourages them to go into quarantine or to seek medical care.

Contact tracers help track how COVID-19 spreads from person to person.

In some places, governments temporarily shut down movie theaters, restaurants, gyms, hotels, hair salons, museums, and coffee shops. They also banned large gatherings. Many nations did not allow international travel.

SOME BUSINESSES CLOSED TEMPORARILY DURING THE PANDEMIC.

Family members and friends stay in touch through video chats.

To keep safe, people stayed home as much as possible. They went to the grocery store less frequently and ordered goods online for home delivery. They used video-chat platforms to talk with friends and family instead of meeting in person. They canceled family vacations.

The cancellations and shutdowns hurt the economy. With fewer customers and less business, many restaurants, hotels, stores, construction companies, airlines, and factories laid off workers. Many companies went out of business. Without jobs, some people couldn't afford to buy enough food or pay rent. Some nations, including the United States, gave unemployment pay to those who lost their jobs. But government programs varied from place to place. In some places, only small numbers of people got unemployment pay.

As businesses shut down or cut staff, some workers lose their jobs.

Chapter 3

THE MOST VULNERABLE

COVID-19 mainly attacks the respiratory system. It first infects the throat and then moves into the lungs. When young, healthy people get infected with the coronavirus, they usually recover quickly. They often have mild symptoms, such as a sore throat or a cough.

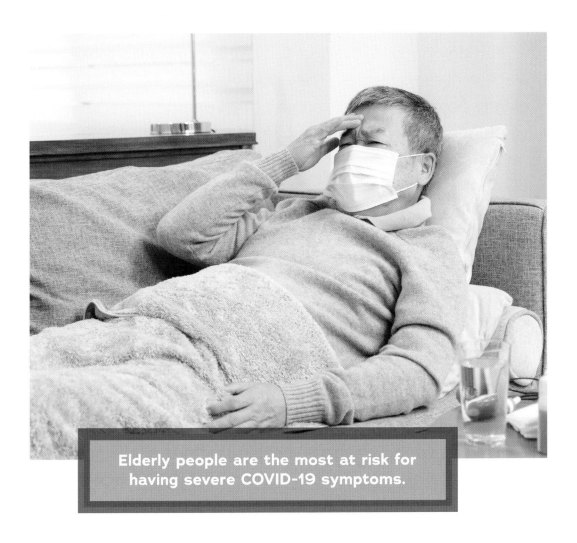

Elderly people are the most at risk for having severe COVID-19 symptoms.

But older people are much more likely to get very sick with COVID-19. As a person ages, their immune system gets weaker. So when an elderly person gets COVID-19, their body might not be able to fight off the infection. If a person already has health problems, such as cancer or heart disease, COVID-19 may make them very sick.

In many nations, the first COVID-19 outbreaks took place in nursing homes. They housed many sick and elderly people. The virus spread from person to person when nursing home staff and residents gathered for meals and social events. By the middle of 2020, about 80 percent of people who had died from COVID-19 in the United States were over 65 years old. Many of them had lived in nursing homes.

Nursing home residents share common areas, making it easy for the virus to spread.

Essential workers risk exposure to the virus to help others buy the food they need.

Hit Hard

Most people tried to avoid getting infected with the coronavirus. That was hard for essential workers. These included grocery clerks, farmworkers, bus drivers, firefighters, doctors, nurses, and paramedics. They had to stay on the job during the pandemic. They couldn't do their jobs from home like many office workers.

Health care workers wore face masks, face shields, gloves, and other personal protective equipment (PPE) when they worked with COVID-19 patients. But it was hard to stay safe on the job. Many doctors, nurses, and other health workers got sick with COVID-19.

PPE helps to protect health care workers who are exposed to the virus on the job.

Dr. Marcella Nunez-Smith

Marcella Nunez-Smith (*below*) is a professor of medicine and public health at Yale University in Connecticut. In 2021, US president Joe Biden appointed her to his COVID-19 advisory board. In this job, Nunez-Smith helps the US government fight the COVID-19 pandemic. She also tries to bring attention to COVID-19 in poor communities. She wants to make sure that every American has equal access to COVID-19 testing, good medical care if they are sick, and vaccinations to prevent illness.

The COVID-19 crisis also hit poor people hard. In the economic downturn, many people lost their jobs and struggled to make rent or house payments. Others had essential jobs at supermarkets, food-processing plants, and nursing homes. They risked infection on the job. In communities around the world, families struggled to social distance at home. This was especially hard in households where kids, parents, and grandparents lived together, and in small homes. In addition, many poor people did not have access to COVID-19 testing or to good medical care if they got sick.

Food banks were more important than ever during the pandemic.

Chapter 4

FIGHTING BACK

In hospitals around the world, health workers struggled to help COVID-19 patients. Many hospitals didn't have enough beds, staff, or equipment to take care of everyone. Some hospitals set up extra structures to house COVID-19 patients.

When COVID-19 attacks the lungs, it can be hard to breathe. In hospitals, doctors used ventilators and oxygen masks to help patients breathe. The virus sometimes attacked other organs, such as the heart or kidneys. Each patient was different, and doctors used different medicines and treatments to help them.

Some patients need oxygen masks to help them breathe.

A RESEARCHER WORKS TO DEVELOP A VACCINE.

▼

Preventing Infection

One of the best ways to fight a disease is to keep people from getting sick with it in the first place. A vaccine builds up the body's defenses against a certain disease. Medical researchers have developed vaccines for many common illnesses. In 2020, they needed to make a vaccine to prevent COVID-19—and they needed it fast.

STEM Spotlight

When germs enter the body, the immune system goes to work. Antibodies attack the invading germs. Special immune cells also fight the invaders. Memory cells "remember" the invaders. If the same type of germ enters the body later, the memory cells recognize it. They alert the rest of the immune system, which makes antibodies more quickly than before. This quick immune response stops the infection before the person gets sick. Vaccines trigger the body's immune response too. But unlike real germs, vaccines don't cause illness.

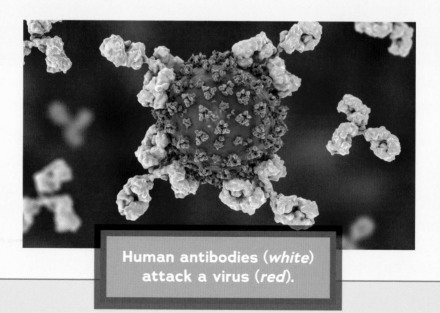

Human antibodies (*white*) attack a virus (*red*).

Normally it takes several years to make a vaccine. But drug companies pushed hard. They made and tested the COVID-19 vaccine in less than a year. By the end of 2020, COVID-19 vaccines were ready for distribution.

Drug companies shipped vaccines to medical centers around the world. Health workers vaccinated the most vulnerable people first. These included essential workers, elderly people, and those with existing health problems. But vaccinating billions of people around the world will take several years.

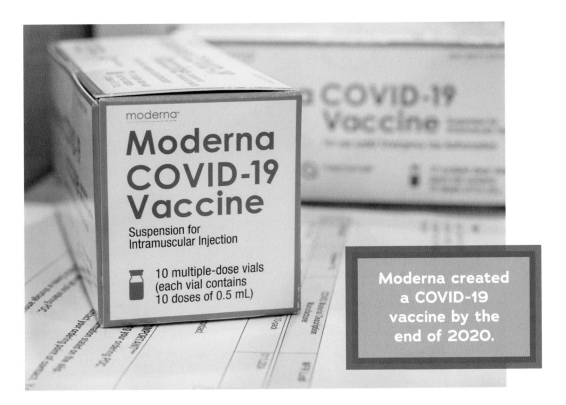

Moderna created a COVID-19 vaccine by the end of 2020.

A health care worker receives their COVID-19 vaccine.

A Post-COVID-19 Future

The COVID-19 vaccine prepares the immune system to fight off the coronavirus. But the virus is changing. To protect people from new strains of the virus, researchers might need to make a new vaccine every year. People might need a yearly COVID-19 vaccine to stay safe.

In the future, new viruses might spread through the air from person to person. If that happens, people will remember the COVID-19 pandemic and take quick action. They will use social distancing, quarantines, contact tracing, vaccination, and other tools to keep the new viruses from spreading. That will help stop new outbreaks before they become pandemics.

Important Dates

December 2019   China reports a disease outbreak in the city of Wuhan.

February 2020   The World Health Organization (WHO) names the disease COVID-19, which is short for "coronavirus disease 2019."

April 2020   The US government encourages all Americans to wear face masks in public to prevent COVID-19 infection.

September 2020   Worldwide, there are more than 1 million deaths due to COVID-19.

November 2020   Drugmakers Moderna and Pfizer announce that they have created effective COVID-19 vaccines.

January 2021   US health organizations administer nearly 1 million COVID-19 vaccinations per day.

February 2021   A vaccine created by Johnson & Johnson is approved for emergency use.

Glossary

antibodies: proteins produced by the immune system to fight infection

essential worker: a person whose work is needed to keep society running

immune system: a network of cells, tissues, and proteins that defend the body against disease

quarantine: a specific time period during which people isolate themselves from others so as not to pass on a disease

respiratory system: the body's breathing organs, including the nose, windpipe, and lungs

social distancing: keeping a certain amount of space between yourself and others, usually 6 feet (2 m), to prevent the spread of disease from person to person

vaccine: a substance that prepares the immune system to fight off an invader, such as a virus

virus: a tiny particle that can infect living cells and cause disease

Learn More

COVID-19: Kids, Here's What You Need to Know
   https://www.canada.ca/en/public-health/services/diseases
   /coronavirus-disease-covid-19/resources-parents-children/kids-need
   -know.html

Farndon, John. *Tiny Killers: When Bacteria and Viruses Attack.*
   Minneapolis: Hungry Tomato, 2017.

Five Things Kids Need to Know about Coronavirus
   https://www.hopkinsmedicine.org/health/conditions-and-diseases
   /coronavirus/5-things-kids-need-to-know-about-coronavirus

The History of Pandemics
   https://www.timeforkids.com/g56/history-pandemics/

Hudak, Heather C. *What Is a Pandemic?* New York: Av2, 2021.

Jackson, Tom. *Pandemic: When Virus Goes Viral.* New York: Kingfisher,
   2021.

Index

Photo Acknowledgments

Image credits: Lightspring/Shutterstock, p.5; Pixel-Shot/Shutterstock, p.6; Everett Collection/Shutterstock, p.7; TJ Brown/Shutterstock, p.8; Tavarius/ZUMA Wire/Shutterstock, p.10; Josep Suria/Shutterstock, p.11; lakshmiprasada S/Shutterstock, p.12; IOANNIS STAMOU/Shutterstock, p.13; Dean Drobot/Daily Express/Hulton Archive/Shutterstock, p.14; ETAJOE/Shutterstock, p.15; aslysun/Philadelphia Inquirer/MCT/Shutterstock, p.17; Nancy Beijersbergen/Atlanta Journal-Constitution/TNS/Shutterstock, p.18; Hispanolistic/Getty Images, p.19; Pordee_Aomboon/Shutterstock, p.20; Biden Transition via CNP/picture alliance/Consolidated News Photos/ZUMA Wire/Newscom, p.21; Spencer Platt/Staff/Getty Images, p.22; DC Studio/Shutterstock, p.24; Pablo Blazquez Dominguez/Stringer/Getty Images, p.25; Kateryna Kon/Shutterstock, p.26; Pool/rosiekeystrokes/Getty Images, p.27; Courtney Hale/Getty Images, p.28

Cover: chayakorn lotongkum/Getty Images